All Around the World

Kelly Cunnane

Illustrated by Pat Tourret

In Kenya, a little boy was eating his breakfast. His name was Kiprotich.
He was sitting on a stool near the door of the hut.
'Please can I have some more maziwa lala?' he asked his mother.
She gave him some more sour milk.

His mother said, 'It is time to go to school.'
Kiprotich washed his face and set off for school.
He walked between the trees along the red road.

Suddenly a monkey jumped down in front of him. It was very big, with long black and white fur.
The monkey showed its teeth.
Kiprotich was frightened.
'Please go away,' he said. 'I mustn't be late for school.'

The monkey ran up a tree.
It jumped from branch to branch.
'Silly monkey!' Kiprotich said and laughed.
He ran down the hill to the school.

In China, a little girl was finishing her lunch. Her name was Liping.
She put her chopsticks across her rice bowl.
'Liping, it is time to go back to school,' her mother said.

Liping went to the bird cage.
'I must say goodbye to Tiny,' she said.
But her pet bird was not in the cage.
'Where has Tiny gone?' she asked.

'You left the door of the cage open,' her mother said. 'He has flown away.'
'I must look for him!' Liping cried.
She was worried. Where could he be?

Just then, the bird flew back into the cage. He started pecking at his seeds. Liping laughed. 'Look,' she said. 'He has come back for his lunch!' She shut the door of the cage. 'Goodbye, Tiny,' she said. 'I'm off to school now.'

In America, another little girl was sitting by a camp fire. Her name was Sara. It was evening.
She called to her mother.
'Mommy, I'm tired. I want to go to bed.'

'I just want to put the baby to bed first,' said her mother.
'You wait by the fire and drink your hot chocolate.'
She took the baby into the tent.

The trees were very dark.
The fire died down.
Sara heard a sound. What was it?
She looked but she could not see anything.

Then her mother came back.
'Mommy!' Sara cried. 'I was frightened!'
Her mother smiled and held Sara's hand.
'Come on, let's go into the tent,' she said. 'I'll read you a bedtime story.'

In America it is night and
Sara is sleeping.
In Kenya it is morning and
Kiprotich is eating his breakfast.
In China it is afternoon and Liping is
sitting at her desk.

In Kenya it is morning, in China it is afternoon and in America it is night. All around the world children are eating, learning and sleeping – just like you!

Activities

Look at the picture. Sara is having her breakfast. It is morning in America.

1. When it is morning in America, it is afternoon in Kenya. What do you think Kiprotich does in the afternoon? Write a sentence and draw a picture.

2. When it is afternoon in Kenya, it is evening in China. What do you think Liping does in the evening? Write a sentence.